HypoGal

HYPOGAL
and
DISABILITY BENEFITS

HypoGal

*Learn How She Received Over
A Million Dollars In Disability Benefits
And How You Can Too...*

BY DAVID GORLICK
WITH FOREWORD FROM
NEW YORK TIMES BEST SELLING AUTHOR,
MICHAEL LEVIN

This publication was created from the author's experiences and designed as a tool to help others in regard to the subject matter covered. The author is not engaged in rendering legal, accounting or other professional services by publishing this book.

If need for any of these services is required, the services of a qualified professional should be sought. The author will not be held responsible for any liability or loss as a result of the information contained in this book.

All notes in this publication to authors, websites, blogs, publications are provided by the author. Real Deal Exchange Corp., has no recommendation or endorsement of this publication nor should any be implied.

Real Deal Exchange Corp.
23052- H Alicia Parkway
PMB # 336
Mission Viejo, CA. 92692

www.HypoGal.com/why-buy-this-book.html

Significant discount for bulk sales are available. Please contact David Gorlick at David@HypoGal.com or 949-380-8000.

ISBN: 061587665X
ISBN 13: 9780615876658

Library of Congress Control Number: 2013922634
HypoGal, Mission Viejo, CA

To My Lisa,

Thank you for allowing me to transfer your voice into my words. You truly create "The Magic".

HypoGal

FOREWORD

by Michael Levin

HypoGal ®

Everyone thinks that disability, like any of life's difficulties, will always happen to the other person. In reality, none of us has immunity from the challenges of life. There's no such thing as a Willy Wonka-like Golden Ticket that will protect us from pain.

Lisa Gorlick a.k.a. HypoGal, whom you'll meet in this extremely powerful, well-organized, and useful book, never expected that she would have the kind of health issues that would entitle her to disability benefits. But as the expression goes, life is what happens when you make other plans.

Lisa did not have a manual when she and her husband, David Gorlick, an attorney, began to unravel the many complexities and roadblocks that stand in the way of the individual who needs to understand the disability system. They had to figure everything out for themselves. The result: Lisa received more than a million dollars in tax-free disability benefits…to which she was abundantly entitled.

With Lisa's feedback David has created what you could call the missing manual to the disability system. You could also call it a gift from above, because if you need disability payments, you probably don't have the strength or the time to figure out all this complicated stuff on your own.

In this short book, you'll discover everything you need to know, every strategy, every form that you must have on the way to applying for and receiving disability benefits. And you'll do so without making yourself sicker or more frustrated by a deeply challenging system.

I urge you to read Lisa's story and walk where she walked. She and her husband David will get you to where you need to go…to receive the benefits you deserve, in the clearest, simplest way possible.

This book might just change your life.

— New York Times best selling author Michael Levin

CONTENTS

HypoGal ®

IF YOU NEED TO APPLY FOR DISABILITY BENEFITS THE FORMS IN CHAPTER THREE WILL ASSIST YOU WITH YOUR APPLICATION.

YOUR INPUT PROVIDES VALUABLE GUIDANCE SO PLEASE REVIEW THIS BOOK.

CHAPTER ONE

The Cost of Being Sick

HypoGal ®

It seems that everyone who applies for disability has a different story but the same common denominator; they are unable to work. A person who applies for disability benefits may feel they are not physically or mentally able to work. Their feeling of inability to work may occur suddenly or develop over a period of time. Some people have the misfortune of being seriously injured in an accident. Whereas, someone else may experience a gradual onset of symptoms before being diagnosed with a life threatening disease.

There are various degrees of disability. The result of an illness or accident contributes to a high percentage of disabled individuals that can live for years and even decades with a disability. A person may also experience a disability for a short time, e.g. weeks, months. Whether your disability is short term or long term, you will need money to survive. The cost of being disabled or living with a long term chronic disease are exorbitant.

1

And, without income or funds from other sources you most likely will not survive a long term disability.

There is little likelihood that your employer will continue to pay you after you have used your sick days. Unfortunately, when you try to recover or live with a disability you will need your income more than ever. Your needs will seem to endlessly expand. You most likely will have to hire people or enlist friends and family to help you. Some of your medical needs may include:

- Someone to accompany you to your doctor's appointments and to be your medical advocate.

- You may not be able to drive. You may need to hire a driver to help you with errands or hire someone to run your errands. These errands may include: grocery shopping, bringing your children to and from school and having your medical prescriptions picked up from the pharmacy.

- Someone to help with your household chores.

- If you have younger children you may need help with daycare.

- If you took care of your lawn then you will probably need to hire a gardener.

- You may need the support of a person to confirm that you have paid your bills correctly. Unfortunately, there will be stacks of medical bills

Ironically, for most people the greatest cost of not being able to work is not from loss of income but from the cost of healthcare bills. Even if you are fortunate enough to have a job with health insurance the cost of being sick can easily cause your household to end up in financial ruins. There is a substantial upward trend in the number of speciality doctors that do not accept health insurance.[1]

Most healthcare plans have a copay or a large deductible.[2] The cost of each copay can quickly amount to a small fortune. It is easy to illustrate how your copay responsibility can cost you hundreds or thousands of dollars each month. In the following example, I will outline how even with fabulous health insurance benefits you may find yourself in financial hardship. I am going to use, "you," in this example. Unfortunately, in this example you have the chronic disease of Lupus. There is some good news, you have a fabulous health insurance plan. Your plan offers a low copay of $25 per medical visit and includes a generous prescription medication plan. The prescription medication plan charges $20 for a generic medication and $40 for a brand medication. Your health insurance plan also offers excellent hospital and lab coverage. The health insurance plan covers 90% of your hospital costs, 80% of lab costs and you do not have a medical deductible.

The example below is an approximation of your monthly medical cost with Lupus. Remember, in this example you have fabulous health insurance:

- You will need an office visit with your rheumatologist to review your labs every eight weeks, $25. Your rheumatologist will most likely order labs before each of your office visits. The copay from your lab work will cost you $40. There is also a high likelihood that your lab copay will increase if you need lab results from a speciality lab. Your diagnosis of the autoimmune disease, Lupus, will most likely cause you to need a team of specialists to treat your disease. Besides your rheumatologist, your medical care team may consist of a dermatologist, ophthalmologist, cardiologist, neurologist and nephrologist. It is not uncommon to have an office visit with each specialist at least once a quarter. These specialists, along with your general practitioner, will cost you approximately $303 per quarter or $101 each month in out of pocket expenses.

- There will be a high probability that a specialist will need to order additional labs or tests. In this example, your cardiologist needs to order labs and a CT Scan. Your out of pocket cost monthly expense for these tests is $140. Regrettably, each month there seems to be a different type of essential test that needs to be ordered.

- Your dermatologist insist that he needs to perform another biopsy of your red inflamed facial rash. The result from a prior biopsy last month was inconclusive. You realize another biopsy will cost you $70 of out of pocket expense. The dermatologist then informs you that he wants you to apply a topical prescription cream to your rash twice a day for at least sixty days. Your doctor then informs you that you need to schedule a follow up appointment in thirty days to determine the effectiveness of the topical cream.

You usually follow up with this doctor every ninety days but this you will need to schedule a follow up appointment for next month. The earlier appointment date will cause you to incur another co-pay. You will also have a $40 out of pocket monthly copay for the newly marketed topical brand prescription the doctor has prescribed for you. Your doctor was firm that he wanted you to use this new brand of topical lotion and a generic form of this medication is not available. Your doctor was sympathetic to your need to save on prescription costs and he gave you a two weeks supply of samples. But, you will still need to fill the prescription because you will not have enough samples.

- During your ophthalmologist appointment your eye doctor confirms that your continuous stinging of your eyes is from moderate to severe dry eyes. You are happy when the doctor informs you that your dry eyes can be treated with over the counter eye drops. Then you find out the price for the small bottle of eye drops is $12. Unfortunately, you will need to use at least one bottle per week. You are stunned at the additional monthly cost of $48 and you begin to feel the out of pocket medical costs spiral out of control.

- You know your medical expenses are exorbitant but your back and neck muscles are in constant spasm. You need to see a massage acupressure therapist but your insurance does not cover this type of physical therapy. Your doctor told you that the massage acupressure therapy may be beneficial to your wellness. You realize that you have significantly fewer muscle spams when your massage therapist works on your body once a week. However, due to out of pocket medical cost you settle on twice a month. The biweekly massage therapy will cost you $200 a month.

As you can see, these medical costs can quickly add up:

EXPENSES	
Doctor Appointments	$101
Labs and Tests	$240
Medications and Prescriptions	$168
Over The Counter Medical Cost	$48
Bi Weekly Massage Therapy	$200
Monthly Out Of Pocket Medical Expenses	$757

After reading through this example you can see how the average monthly cost of $757 may seem like a fairly predictable forecast. However, if you are chronically ill there is nothing predictable about medical costs. The monthly out of pocket cost of $757 does not include the cost of any supplemental vitamins that you may decide to include in your diet.

The additional medical expenses seem to never end. I sadly recall the medical experience of Sally, a young diabetic woman. Sally told me about her frustrations to have her $850 ambulance ride covered by her health insurance provider. She told me that one morning while she was grocery shopping she had fainted and lost conscientiousness.

A grocery store clerk had phoned 911 and an ambulance was sent to the grocery store. When the ambulance attendants checked her vital signs they noticed she wore a medical identification bracelet. Her medical identification bracelet stated that she had Diabetes and Adrenal Insufficiency. The ambulance attendants started her an IV drip and rushed her to the closest hospital.

Sally told me that she was in and out of consciousness when she arrived at the hospital. She was grateful that an Emergency Room doctor had quickly injected her with life saving medication. A few hours after her treatment in the Emergency Room she was transferred to a hospital room. Sally knew she was fortunate that she was able to leave the hospital and return home the next day.

About two weeks after Sally's hospital stay the piles of medical bills began to arrive. She had never imagined that she would be billed $850 for the life saving ambulance ride from the grocery store to the hospital. When she phoned her health insurance company they informed her that the ambulance transportation was not covered. The insurance company representative told her that the ambulance service she used was not within their network. She was stunned by the unfairness and absurdity of the insurance company's decision. Despite over a dozen phone calls to different managers and two letters to their legal department, her outcome remained the same. She was still held responsible for the ambulance bill.

Unfortunately, the $850 ambulance bill was only one of the many medical bills from her medical crisis in the grocery store. The hospital labs, Emergency Room doctors, hospital doctors and hospital each billed her separately. She was upset to discover that you could receive so many bills from a one day hospital stay. After her health care insurance paid the claims on her one day hospital stay she owed over $1,700 in out of pocket cost.

Sally's health insurance paid 90% of in patient hospital costs, doctor's services and 80% for tests and lab work. The following is a breakdown of what Sally was billed:[3]

1 DAY HOSPITAL STAY	
10% From Hospital Room	$250
10% From E.R. Doctors	$280
10% From Hospital Doctors	$90
100% Of The Ambulance Cost	$850
20% Test and Lab Work	$240
TOTAL COST FROM A ONE DAY HOSPITAL STAY	$1,710

Sally incurred $1710 in out of pocket medical cost from her one day of hospital care. After four months her insurance company still had not covered any portion of her $850 ambulance transportation.

The example above demonstrates how even a person with excellent healthcare insurance coverage can incur extremely high out of pocket medical costs. This example is not out of the ordinary. Even with these staggering out of pocket medical costs, Sally knew she was fortunate to have health insurance. Not every employer offers health insurance and if you become seriously ill you may lose your health insurance coverage.

If your health insurance is provided through your employer, you may lose your coverage if you are no longer able to work. You may feel you need to leave your job because you are too sick to safely work. If your health insurance is provided by your employer then you will most likely be able to participate in COBRA insurance.

COBRA is the acronym for Consolidated Omnibus Budget Reconciliation Act. Congress passed the COBRA health benefit provisions in 1986. The law amends the Employee Retirement Income Security Act, the Internal Revenue Code and the Public Health Service Act to provide continuation of group health coverage under certain conditions.

These conditions give certain former employees, retirees, spouses former spouses, and dependent children the right to temporary continuation of health coverage at group rates. The monthly rate for COBRA Group health coverage participants is usually significantly more expensive than health coverage for active employees. Most employers contribute to a portion of the health insurance premium for active employees. Whereas, COBRA participants generally have to pay the entire premium.[4]

The COBRA health premiums are generally substantially higher than private insurance. Many people have found their COBRA rate to be three to four times the cost of their original insurance. If a health insurance company does offer you one of their plans a higher premium is usually reflected in the monthly rate.

When faced with the high health insurance premiums some people may decide to forgo COBRA health insurance. Some people may feel the high cost of COBRA or private health insurance will cause too much financial stress on their household budget. Whereas, other people may feel that they are healthy and it is worth the risk of being uninsured. However, unless your household is already in complete financial ruin, health insurance is a necessity. The peace of mind from including health insurance in your family budget is priceless.

CHAPTER TWO

HypoGal Disabled, Her Story

My wife's medical odyssey has been a humbling, terrifying and at times empowering journey. In this chapter I will share with you her story as voiced in her own words. It is my hope that my wife's story will provide some guidance and assistance for those coping with a chronic illness. Here is her story:

My name is Lisa Gorlick a.k.a. HypoGal. I had always envisioned a disabled person with a physical handicap. It had not crossed my mind that a person could become disabled by a chronic disease. I was certainly aware that people became ill with life threatening diseases. However, I had never given much thought to life with a chronic disease until it became my story.

My story of life with a chronic disease began with the birth of my second daughter. After my daughter was delivered via C-Section my body began to slowly deteriorate. At first, I thought I was just tired and my body was fatigued. As the months passed

I could not stop my weight loss. My thick brunette hair begun to fall out by the handful, my body continuously throbbed with pain, everything I ate went right through me and I became depressed.

I went from doctor to doctor to find a diagnosis. Each doctor told me that my tests were normal and I was just depressed. I felt like a broken record as I conveyed to doctor after doctor that I was depressed because I was very sick. I could feel that my body had ceased to correctly function and I suffered from more than depression.

As the months passed my body became weaker and weaker. I was no longer able to take care of my girls and we had to hire a full time nanny. I realized that even with my dire health situation, my family was fortunate to have incredible health insurance. On the other hand, I was all to aware that my terrific health insurance would disappear within a year. I had accepted a generous buy out package from my large corporate employer. The corporate buy out package I had accepted included a lengthy extension of my salary and health care benefits.

My husband and I were thrilled that my healthcare insurance would enable us to keep our incredible health insurance for an extended period of time. We were aware that it would be very expensive to privately replicate my large corporate benefit package.

My former employer had offered a phenomenal benefit package. Their benefit package included different options for healthcare insurance, life insurance and disability insurance. I had always taken advantage of their generous benefit programs. I had enrolled in their health insurance, life insurance and disability insurance benefit programs.

I had chosen to purchase the Preferred Provider Organization (PPO) rather than the Health Maintenance Program (HMO) because the insurance offered a wider selection of doctors. Unlike the HMO program, The PPO program allowed me to receive healthcare from any doctor within their preferred network. I would not need a referral from my primary doctor before I was able to see a specialist. The financial downside was that my PPO annual deductible and co-pay did cost more.

The life insurance policy was an easy decision for me to make. I chose the maximum pay out. The life insurance premium was a small monthly amount and my family would be given additional financial protection.

Oh, how I wish I would have chosen to enroll in the maximum pay out for disability insurance. As I reflect back, I realize I was too naive to think that I would ever need a disability policy. The main reason I had signed up for this benefit was due to the wise words of a former coworker and friend. My insightful coworker had told me about the importance of disability insurance. In an extremely serious tone she had vocalized to me the biggest insurance oversights young adults may make is not having a disability insurance policy. She then went on to state alarming statistics about becoming disabled as an adult. She said that almost a quarter of adults would become disabled during their lives. That alarming statistic equated to just about one in four adults would become disabled for a period of time in their adult life. That statistic was alarming to me.

I suspected that my coworker's statistics were a bit exaggerated. I just could not envision that one out of four of my adult friends would become disabled. It turns out my coworker's statement was correct and I was sorely mistaken. According to The Social Security Administration in 2013, it states that just over 33.3% of today's 20 year olds will become disabled for some period of time before they retire.[1] Surprising, only a small percentage of disabilities are the result of an injury. A large majority of disabilities are caused by numerous illnesses.

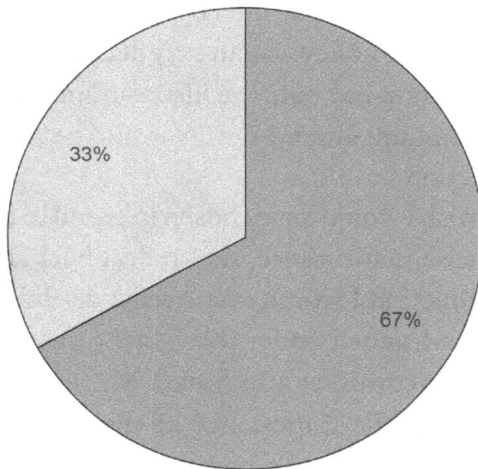

- 1 IN 3 ADULTS WILL BECOME DISABLED

- 2 OUT OF 3 WILL NOT BE DISABLED

During our company enrollment for disability benefits her words about disability statistics did echo through my mind, just not loud enough. I still found it difficult to believe the high number of individuals that would become disabled, especially someone like myself. Except for allergies my entire life had been relatively healthy and I was young. But, her wise words about disability insurance did resonate in the back of my mind. So, I decided that even though disability insurance would be a waste of funds I should explore the options.

As I recall, my employer had offered several choices of disability insurance coverage. I believe the options were 50%, 75% and 100% of your salary if you were to become disabled for more than ninety days. I remember the debate inside my head whether to spend an additional twenty dollars a month for 100% coverage. Due to what I thought was a likely waste of money I immediately eliminated 100% coverage. I then waffled between the choice of 75% coverage and 50% of coverage. I began to check the box for 75% of coverage but then decided to check the 50% of coverage box. I justified checking the 50% coverage box with a number of excuses, particularly denial. After a ten second debate in my mind, I concluded that if I were to become disabled my needs would be limited. I could not have been more mistaken. Unfortunately, I have learned that if you are to become disabled you will need your income more than ever. Your ongoing medical expenses seem to never end.

There have been many days when I think about all the frivolous things I have spent money on but I did not want to spend the extra twenty dollars a month to maximize my disability benefits. I was just naive to believe that I would always have good health. At the time I signed up for disability insurance I seriously believed that if I were to become disabled I would most likely die within a year of my injury. I write injury because I was in complete denial that people can live for decades with a serious illness. A large majority of people on disability are not from injury but from a serious illness.[2]

It was during my ten month buy out period when I applied for disability benefits. My buy out agreement stated I would receive my salary directly deposited into my bank account for a ten month time period. I would also be entitled to my health insurance and life insurance for that time period. Disability insurance was not mentioned nor included. I truly believe karma played a role in what happened next.

One afternoon before my buy out period had begun, I went to my mailbox and I pulled out the usual enormous stack of mail. I noted that most of the mail looked like it consisted of junk mail. I brought the large stack of mail inside my home and I began to separate the mail into two piles.

One mail pile consisted of junk mail and the other pile consisted of bills and personal notes. The mail I placed in the first pile, I usually left unopened and immediately tossed into the trash. As I quickly sorted the mail into two piles, I glanced twice at a small non business size envelope. The envelope struck me as odd. The small envelope had an out of state return address and did not include a business name. Across the front of the envelope was a diagonal bold red stamped message that read "Important Information". Surprisingly, I did not toss out this envelope into the junk mail pile.

This letter marked, "Important Information" was one of the last pieces of mail I opened. The letter inside the envelope was from a major disability insurance company that claimed to underwrite the disability policy for my large corporate employer. The letter stated for a small fee they would extend my disability benefits during my buy out period. A gut feeling instinctively gave me insight to explore this, "Important Information" solicitation.

I phoned my employer's Human Resource Department to verify the information mailed to me was legitimate. Upon confirmation that the letter was credible I sent the insurance company their requested premium. I believe the fee to extend my benefits was under forty dollars per month. That small envelope with its diagonal red stamped marketing slogan forever changed my life. It was during my buy out period that the symptoms of my undiagnosed Sheehan Syndrome began to deteriorate my body. As my body deteriorated the stacks of medical bills began to accumulate. I worried that if I did not pass soon I would leave my family a mountain of medical debt.

As my body went in and out of consciousness, I directed my husband to phone the insurance company and inquire about my disability insurance extension. The insurance company informed my husband that I needed to complete a couple of forms to begin a claim. Two weeks after my forms were submitted to the insurance company my disability benefits began to arrive weekly.

My husband and I were relieved to receive the disability funds. Shortly after we began to receive the monthly checks we realized that the income was not taxed. We immediately checked with our accountant and we learned that disability benefits purchased with private funds are not taxable. If I had paid my disability insurance payment with funds deducted from my paycheck then my benefits would have been taxed. Since I did not pay my disability insurance policy in pre taxed dollars I was able to receive tax free benefits.

However, my entire disability income did not remain tax free. I was a bit bewildered when an attorney from the insurance company phoned me. At first, I informed him that I did not need his services. He then immediately interrupted me and informed me of the legalities of a line item located in the terms of my disability policy. This line item term in my policy allowed the insurance company to seek Social Security benefits on my behalf.

I was confused when the attorney mentioned Social Security. At the time, I believed Social Security Benefits were a small resource you received in your sixties. I was not aware that Social Security provided a vehicle for disabled people to obtain medical insurance. My husband and I had begun to worry about my health insurance situation. My health insurance would end in less than a year. We both knew that with my expensive medical costs I would most likely join the millions of other uninsurable individuals.

The attorney for the insurance company informed me that I immediately needed to submit a Social Security Benefits Disability Application. I was too exhausted to confirm my options and I continued to have a fifteen minute phone interview with him. After our phone call, my husband faxed the attorney the signed authorization forms. These forms authorized the attorney to file a Social Security Disability application on my behalf.

A couple of days later a woman from my local Social Security Administration Office phoned me. Unfortunately, when she phoned me I was experiencing a difficult day. The fatigue and dizziness from Sheehan's Syndrome had made it almost impossible for me to sit up in bed. I was also having immense difficulties forming words and my speech was often delayed. Fortunately, my inability to promptly answer the Social Security woman's questions did not deter her from completing our interview. During our twenty minute phone interview she focused on dates of my hospitalization, medication, the dates of my doctors appointments and the name and phone number of each of my doctors.

Even though my brain seemed to operate at an extremely slow speed I was able to give the woman from the Social Security office the information she requested. Fortunately, I had already created a timeline of my hospitalizations, a list of my doctors information and dates of appointments. I have found that having a printed copy of your health timeline, medication list and doctors information can be a valuable tool.

I was still confused about the information the attorney had told to me. Thankfully, the woman from the Social Security office was very patient with me and she provided me with a wealth of information. She informed me that if I qualified for Social Security Disability Insurance than I would automatically be enrolled in the Medicare health insurance 24 months after my SSDI began.

She went on to patiently explain to me that after a 24 month period on SSDI a person is automatically enrolled in Medicare health insurance. Once a person is on Medicare health insurance they are eligible to acquire a prescription coverage plan through Medicare.[3] My children would also receive a Social Security Benefit monthly payment until they reached the age of 18.

She also explained that a divorced spouse, spouse or adult child disabled before the age of 22 may qualify for Social Security Benefits. The amount of funds a family can receive is limited.[4] Your monthly disability benefits are based on your lifetime average earnings covered by Social Security.[5]

She then advised me that Social Security Disability Insurance (SSDI) benefits varies for each person. The amount of Social Security Disability Insurance benefits would be based on my average lifetime earnings before my disability began. The monthly amount of SSDI I received would not be based on the severity of the disability. Also, if my disability progressed my monthly Social Security Disability Insurance would remain the same.[6]

She went on to say that if I was eligible for Social Security Insurance (SSI) and Veteran Benefits (VA) I would still be able to apply for Social Security Disability Insurance. However, if I received government regulated disability benefits, such as temporary state disability benefits or workers' comp benefits it would affect my Social Security Disability Insurance. She then conveyed that a person may not receive more than 80% of the average amount you earned before you became disabled in SSDI and other disability benefits. If you do, your SSDI benefit will be reduced.[7]

She also educated me on the Federal program Social Security Income (SSI). This program provides a monthly payment to people who have limited income and have few resources. To be eligible for SSI you may not have a financial net worth more than $2,000 and $3,000 if you are married. A person must have at least one of the following to be eligible for SSI:

- Have a medical condition that prevents you from working and is expected to last at least one year or result in death.

- You are partially blind or completely blind

- You are 65 years of age or older

- The basic Supplemental Security Income (SSI) is the same nationwide in 2013. If you qualify you will receive:

- $710 for one person each month

- $1,066 for a couple each month[8]

Not everyone receives the same basic amount of Supplemental Security Income. You may receive additional income if you reside in a state that gives additional funds to the Federal SSI payment. Your SSI monthly funds may be decreased if you or your family has access to other resources, e.g., pension. To receive Supplemental Security Income you a United States citizen you still may able to receive Supplemental Security Income.

I also learned private disability insurance payments will not affect the financial award of my Social Security Disability Insurance benefits. A disabled person is allowed to collect private disability insurance and Social Security Disability Insurance benefits concurrently.[10]

When I ended the Social Security Office phone interview I was utterly relieved. The stress of not being able to obtain health insurance had placed an enormous amount of stress on my already exhausted body. I knew my medical bills for that year had already reached the six figure range. It became very apparent to me how many families may end up in bankruptcy from medical costs. I was happy to learn there were Federal programs in place for disabled individuals that had little financial means.

Even through I was deathly sick I was comforted by the fact my illness fit the parameters of being disabled under Federal Social Security. Federal Social Security will only pay benefits to people who cannot work because they have a medical condition that is expected to last at least one year or result in death. Federal law requires this very strict definition of disability. While some programs give money to people with partial disability or short-term disability, Social Security does not.[11]

For the state agency to decide that you are disabled, your medical condition must significantly limit your ability to do basic work activities. These activities include walking, sitting and remembering. You must not be able to participate in basic work activities for at least one year. If your medical condition is not that severe, the state agency will not consider you disabled. If your condition is that severe, the state agency goes on to further review your application.[12]

It had been about three weeks after the woman from the Social Security Office submitted my SSDI application that she phoned our home. Her news was joyous to my much frazzled husband. She informed our family that I had been approved for Social Security Disability Insurance benefits. She told my husband that my benefits would be back dated to the day when I first became sick. The Social Security Disability Insurance benefits for my daughters would also be back dated. The funds from the Social Security office arrived about two weeks later. I would like to write that I was ecstatic about the wonderful news but I was too sick to care. My body had failed me and the feeling of hopelessness had engulfed me.

My husband, David, tried desperately to help me move forward. He reassured me that my private disability insurance policy provided enough to offset my endless medical costs. He also familiarized himself with the terms of my disability contract.

The terms of most private disability policies are most flexible than Social Security Disability Insurance.

The example below illustrates the differences between private disability insurance and Social Security Disability Insurance.

This example shows what happens after Bill the dentist injures his fingers. Dr. Bill earns the average dental income of $12,400 a month or $149,000 a year.[12] Unfortunately, Bill fractured two of his right fingers while boogie boarding with his son at the beach. The injury occurred as Bill and his son collided near the shoreline. Bill's son accidentally kicked his right hand as he struggled out of the water. As a result of the injury Bill was unable to practice dentistry.

Fortunately, Dr. Bill has private disability insurance. The private disability insurance pays 75% of Bill's monthly income 90 days after he is unable to practice dentistry. The Social Security Disability Benefits would pay Doctor Bill $0 after 90 days and $0 after the first year he is unable to work from his hand injury. Social Security Disability Benefits will not be paid to an individual that is able to work. Doctor Bill injured his two fingers but he is able to work a different type of job.

Remember, Federal Social Security will only pay benefits to people who cannot work because they have a medical condition that is expected to last at least one year or result in death. Federal law requires this very strict definition of disability. While some programs give money to people with partial disability or short-term disability, Social Security does not.[13] In contrast, if Doctor Bill had private disability insurance he most likely would not have to seek out another field of employment.[14]

The chart below shows that Doctor Bill receives a 75% monthly payment from his private disability insurance policy. The chart compares the differences between private disability insurance benefits and Social Security Disability Benefits. Unfortunately, Doctor Bill's hand injury was substantial and he will require longer than 90 days to heal.

This chart compares monetary funds Doctor Bill would receive if he is unable to perform dentistry:

Number of Days Unable To Perform Dentistry	Monthly Funds From Private Disability Insurance	Monthly Funds From Social Security Disability Benefits
91 Days	$9,312	$0
121Days	$18,624	$0
151Days	$27,936	$0
181 Days	$55,872	$0
362 Days	$83,808	$0

Since Doctor Bill had a private disability insurance policy he will be paid $9,312 a month after he is not able to work for 90 days. Doctor Bill will receive $9,312 a month tax free since he paid for his private disability insurance policy with after tax dollars.

If Doctor Bill did not have private disability insurance then his family would have suffered sufficient financial consequences.

Unfortunately, Bill's fractured two fingers did not heal well. Bill had surgery twice to repair the his fingers. He was not able to perform dentistry for 14 months. Below is a comparison of funds that Bill would have received if he was unable to perform his dentistry for 14 months:

Months Unable To Work	Monthly Funds From A Private Disability Insurance	Monthly Funds From Social Security Disability Insurance
14 Months	$102,432	$0

Remember, in order for the state agency to decide that you are disabled, your medical condition must significantly limit your ability to do basic work activities such as walking, sitting and remembering for at least one year. If your medical condition is not that severe, the state agency will not consider you disabled.[15]

I was fortunate to have private disability insurance. In my private disability insurance policy there was a term that stated, I must apply for Social Security Disability Insurance if my disability is long term. The insurance company included this term within my policy as a way to reduce their payout. When I was approved for Social Security Disability Benefits my SSDI monthly payment replaced part of my private disability insurance monthly payout. SSDI funded part of my long term disability insurance. I believe the SSDI requirement in my policy term is the reason my insurance company hired on attorney on my behalf. With the assistance from my attorney I was awarded SSDI benefits. However, if I was denied SSDI benefits my insurer would still be required to pay 100% of my benefits.

The SSDI program has enabled me to participate in the healthcare program that Social Security Disability Insurance offers. I have received over a million dollars in medical benefits through Social Security Disability Insurance. The cost of my health insurance coverage is approximately $250 a month. Each month SSDI deducts my health insurance premiums from my SSDI payment. I also have Medicare prescription coverage but I do pay an annual $5000 prescription deductible and a co-pay on all prescriptions.

Each year I enroll in one of the most expensive Medicare prescription plans. I have chosen to enroll in the most costly plan because of the high cost of my numerous medications. I was aware that even with the highest premium prescription plan I would still hit the Doughnut Hole.

So what does the phase, "Doughnut Hole" mean? The "Doughnut Hole" refers to a gap in prescription drug coverage under Medicare Part D. In 2013, once you reach $2,970 in prescription drug costs (which include both your share of covered drugs and the amount paid by your insurance), you will be in the coverage gap.

In 2013, you will receive a 50 percent discount on brand-name drugs and a 14 percent discount on generic prescription drugs while you are in the coverage gap. When your total out-of-pocket costs reach $4,750, you qualify for "catastrophic coverage." Once you have paid $4,750 you are responsible for only 5 percent of your prescription drug costs for the rest of the year.[16]

Due to the extreme costs of my prescriptions I can hit the Donut Hole in as little as two months. The retail cost for one of my medications is $3,900 per month. I have been on this brand of medication for over ten years. It is easy to calculate how my annual out of pocket prescription costs can reach $9,500 per year.

Although I am enrolled in a terrific prescription plan, I still end up paying an average of $800 a month in prescription costs. Each time I have a doctor's visit, testing, lab work, an operation or hospital stay my bills are submitted to Medicare for payment. Even through Medicare covers a sufficient amount of my healthcare needs, I am always billed my co-payment portion. My average co-payments from Medicare are approximately $400 a month. In addition, I spend about $120 a month for an out of network medical specialist.

I spend roughly, $120 each month for my vitamins and supplements. My twice a month acupressure massage therapy costs me $200. If you include my vitamins, supplements and acupressure massage therapy then my medical costs would be approximately $1,880 a month. The chart below outlines my approximate monthly and annual medical expenses.

Approximate Medical Cost	Per Month	Annual Costs
Medical Insurance	$240	$2,880
Co-Pays	$400	$4,800
Medication	$800	$9,600
Vitamins and Supplements	$120	$2,400
Massage Therapy	$200	$2,400
Out Of Network Physicians	$100	$1,200
Total Medical Cost	$1,880	$22,560

Unfortunately, the expenses of being sick are not only medical costs but my physical shortage of energy. I am not able to work. I have to hire people to help me with simple everyday chores. My husband has assumed most of the driving responsibilities and our family schedule has to be planned around how I feel. I spend approximately $600 a month for services that I cannot physically accomplish. When my children were younger I spent $1500 a month to have full time daily help with my children.

I am all too aware there is not a way to accurately calculate the true cost of my chronic illness. I cannot place a price on the days I have lost to my illness. I wish I could have been there to raise my newborn daughter or to play in the park with my oldest daughter. But, I do realize how my Social Security Disability Benefits and my private disability insurance have enabled me to watch my children grow into young people.

I do receive a tax free monthly payment from my private insurance company. Even though my Social Security Disability Insurance benefits are taxed my SSDI benefits enable most of my health care needs to be met.

Chronically sick individuals who do not have private disability insurance do not have the luxury of having an attorney hired and paid for on their behalf. If you are chronically ill and you need to apply for Social Security Disability Insurance you may need to hire your own attorney. You should be aware of the following:

- It is against the law for a Social Security lawyer to collect an upfront fee from you.

- A lawyer may only collect a small fee for postage and to obtain copies of your medical records.

- Your Social Security attorney fee may not exceed $6,000 or 25% of your backpay, whichever is less.

- Even if your case goes on for years your attorney will not receive payment unless you win.[17]

You may feel overwhelmed by the process of obtaining an attorney. Nevertheless, you should know the following about the attorney you plan to hire:

- How many years the attorney has practiced Social Security law.

- If the attorney practices any other areas of law beside Social Security. You want a lawyer that specializes in Social Security.

- You should know if the attorney will handle your case or if your case will be given to one of their associates.

- The number of Social Security cases the attorney has worked on and the number of cases the attorney has won.

- Will the attorney to able to provide you with a list of references.

Most insurance companies hire successful Social Security law firms to look out for their best financial interest. You need to be sure you hire the best Social Security attorney to handle your claim. You should definitely consider obtaining counsel if your SSDI claim is denied.

Approximately 70% of all SSDI applicants are denied on their first application. Many of these claims are denied because the application was not completed correctly. Whereas, other applicants may be denied because they have submitted applications twice. Social Security will not proceed with your application if you have a prior application submitted. In

2012, Social Security Disability received 2,820,812 applicants and awarded 979,973 claims. The number of Social Security Disability Insurance awarded in 2012 was 4% less than in 2011. In addition, some of these awarded applicants may have taken years to process.[18]

After I learned the high percentage of SSDI applications that are denied benefits the first time, I realized how fortunate I was to have my SSD approved on the first submittal. My ability to receive SSDI has allowed me to participate in the Medicare health insurance and prescription plan.

A person that receives Social Security Disability Benefits for 24 months is automatically eligible for Medicare. When I first became ill I was fortune to have COBRA health insurance and then after 24 months on SSDI I became eligible for Medicare. The medical and prescription benefits I have received from Medicare have allowed me and my family to financial survive.

Since 2003 I have received more than a million dollars in disability benefits. When I refer to disability benefits that I have received I have included healthcare insurance benefits, prescription costs, SSDI payments and disability payments from my private disability policy.

The following is a chart that illustrates an approximate amount of disability benefits I have received since 2003:

SOURCE OF MY DISABILITY BENEFITS	BENEFITS RECEIVED
Private Disability Insurance	$316,800
SSDI Social Security	$528,400
Health Insurance Benefits	> $500,000
Prescription Policy	> $500,000
Total Benefits Received	$1,845,200

There have been numerous years when my healthcare costs have exceeded $100,000. I have received over $500,000 in medical benefits through my Medicare health insurance benefit. The $500,000 costs in medical benefits does not include the cost of my prescription medications. The retail cost of my prescriptions since 2003 has easily exceeded $500,000. In addition to over a million dollars in costs covered by my health insurance and prescription plan, I have been fortunate to have received more than $700,000 in disability insurance payments.

My disability benefits are paid to me monthly. The disability benefits consist of entitled funds from SSDI and my private disability policy. I do think, wow, when I recall that I have received more than $700,000 in monetary benefits. I believe $700,000 is a substantial amount of money. However, if you break down the costs of being sick each year you realize how quickly the funds evaporate. Each year I spend over $25,000 on medical costs. I do realize that I am blessed to receive enough funds from my private insurance disability to pay my medical costs and contribute to our household expenses.

Unfortunately, I am unable to maintain the daily upkeep of my home and I need additional support. I am only able to grocery shop when I feel a spurt of energy and I have to forgo shopping for the best price points on items. There have been dozens of times when I have had to hire others to help me with my daily errands.

My disability benefits will continue until I am able to work full time. Each year my private insurance company requires my doctor to validate my medical condition. Social Security Disability Insurance also requires me to annually complete their medical and financial questionnaire. The Social Security Disability Insurance questionnaire wants me to confirm that the funds my children received were used to take care of their needs.

The conditions of returning to employment are different between my private disability insurance policy and SSDI. My private disability insurance policy is paid out to me if I am unable to perform a like job similar to my prior position. Whereas, Social Security requires that you are unable to work any job.[19] Sadly, I do not have the physical strength to maintain any type of work. Through the years my health has further deteriorated and I am unable to explore any job options.

My private disability insurance policy has allowed my financial situation to be more comfortable than hundreds of thousands of other chronically ill individuals. Many chronically ill people are too sick to work and they have limited financial resources. Medical costs involve more than half of all bankruptcies filed since 2009.[20] I have no doubt that without access to health insurance coverage, prescription coverage and disability payments our household would have been an unfortunate statistic.

I am grateful that my private disability policy has enabled my family to ward off bankruptcy and maintain a comfortable standard of living. I will be forever thankful that I responded to that small envelope stamped with the red diagonal comment, "Important Information."

CHAPTER THREE

Disability Insurance

HypoGal ®

Our family life coping with a chronic illness has become a series of medical stories. I recall one of Lisa's experiences at a medical support forum. She sat down next to a middle aged man during a lunch break at the forum. From one look at this man it was apparent that he had a chronic illness. His hazel eyes were sunken and dark half moon circles surrounded his eyes. It looked as if someone had filled the hanging half moon circles under his eyes with a black Sharpie Pen. His premature gray hair appeared to have a dry straw texture and muscle waste hung from his face, arms and stomach region. Even though he was dressed in a fancy sweater and pressed pants his appearance screamed of exhaustion. He meekly smiled at my wife as she inquired if she could sit down next to him. She sensed he needed an open ear. He told Lisa during their lunch break that he endured continuous health battles, how he prays for a cure to his illness and his strong desire to move out of his parents house.

He sadly told Lisa the reason he lives at home was due to lack of funds. He went on to tell her that his parents did not understand his life with an invisible disease and they thought he was fat and lazy. He said they thought he was lazy because he laid around the house all day and he was continuously let go from numerous part time jobs.

Lisa went on to inquire about his work history. He told her his job history was filled with large gaps and that he was let go from positions because he was too sick to work. But, he knew he needed to work to afford to live and pay for his medication. He went on to say that due to his lack of funds he often went without his much needed medication. He felt defeated, frustrated and overwhelmed by what he perceived as a hopeless downward spiral.

She asked him if he had ever applied for disability benefits and he looked at her with tear swollen eyes and told her that he was just recently denied. Lisa asked him why he was denied benefits and he muttered, lifestyle. She questioned his lifestyle response. After a small hesitation, he blurted out that he was too embarrassed to tell the woman at the Social Security Office that he felt so sick that he sat around the house all day. So, instead of the truth he told the Social Security Administration Office representative that his typical day consisted of going on walks, watching television and interacting on his computer.

Lisa's heart sank for him. She told him that he did not choose to have this disease but he can choose how to best navigate his life. She then conveyed to him that he needed to be honest about the severity of his health disabilities. Lisa also told him that it was imperative that he put together an action plan.

Lisa then began to reflect on her disability application process and the disability experiences of others. She decided the following check list was helpful when she applied for disability benefits:

- You need to be organized and detailed. Keep all the information from your illness together. A three ring binder with divider tabs may help you with the organization of your records.

- Note the date when you first became ill.

- Keep a timeline of all doctor appointments and hospital stays.

- Have a list that contains your doctors' information. The list should include their name, address, phone number and your doctors' speciality, e.g. endocrinologist.

- If you have neighbors or friends that are familiar with your disability struggles then you should ask them to complete a form that looks similar to this form:

Statement From Friends and Family

(1) Name: _____
                    Your Name (Friend or Family Member)

Date: _____   _____   _____
              Month   Day   Year

Street Address _____

_____
                City   State   Zip Code

(2) I have known _____
                          The Person Who Is Submitting This Form

   for _____
                          Period of Time

(3) I know _____
                      Person Who is Submitting This Form

   from _____
            Family/ Friend/ Neighbor/ Work/ School/ Church

Statement From Friends and Family

(4) I have noticed the following changes in their personality and/ or physical appearance from the time of _____, 20 _____ to _____, 20 _____

(5) Some of the changes in their personality and/or physical appearance are:

Name Printed _____

Signature _____

Dated _____   _____   _____
                   Month   Day   Year

Phone Number _____   _____
                  Area Code   Phone Number

Street Address _____

_____
        City   State   Zip Code

If the person has numerous remarks about your personality and/or physical appearance you may want them to write, "See Attachment" in area (5) and attach a separate page labeled #5 that details your changes. The letter should be concise, give examples and dates.

If a close neighbor has noticed that you have been too sick to mow your lawn or tend to your garden over a certain time period then they should include this in the area 5 Remark section. An example may read as follows:

Every Saturday morning for the last nine years, my neighbor (Your Name) has mowed their lawn and tended to their vegetable garden. However, since the start of this summer I have noticed (Your Name) has not had the strength to keep up with their lawn maintenance.

If a family member has helped you with errands, chores and is aware that you are too sick to maintain your job, then your example may want to read like this:

My sister, (Your Name) devotedly washed her family's laundry, grocery shopped, ran two miles every morning and worked forty hours a week. Sadly, over the past year I have watched my sister's health decline. Her husband now does all the laundry. I shop for their family's groceries and run many of the family's errands. Our mother watches her twin seven year olds girls after school. My sister has had to give up a job she loved and she spends her day in bed or on the couch. She is too weak to sit up and she usually only showers twice a week with my help.

The Statement of Attending Physician is on the following page. Your doctor may charge you a small fee to complete this form. However, even if your doctor charges you a fee it is a good idea to have this form or a form similar to this form completed.

A judge and/or the insurance company will be better equipped to approve your application if a complete summary of your medical condition is conveyed by your doctor.

If you have your doctor complete the Physician Statement Form in this book it will assist a judge or insurance company representative in evaluating your medical condition. A judge or insurance representative may not be able to fully interpret the complexity of your medical records. A summary of your medical condition will give a judge or insurance representative a concise overview from a medical expert.

Statement Of Attending Physician

(1) Patient: _____

Date of Birth: _____ _____ _____
                        Month   Day   Year

Present Condition: _____

Subjective Symptoms:

Objective Findings:

_____

(2) Please list ICD9 #

_____

(3) Treatment

(3.1) Date of First Visit: Month _____ Day _____ 20 _____

(3.2) Date of Last Visit: Month _____ Day _____ 20 _____

(3.3) Frequency of Visits: Weekly Monthly Other

(3.4) Progress: Recovered Improved Unimproved

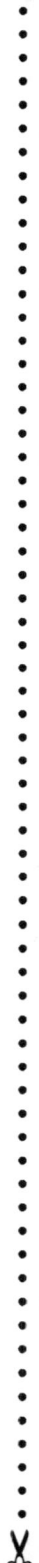

(4) Extent of Disability

(4.1) For Any Occupation?　Yes　No

(4.2) For His/Her Regular Occupation?　Yes　No

(4.3) Is patient now totally disabled?　Yes　No

(4.4) Does the disability or impairment prevent the patient from standing for six to eight hours?　Yes　No

(4.5) If the patient can stand at all, and if so for how long?

(4.6) Does the disability or impairment prevent the patient from sitting upright for six to eight hours?　Yes　No

(4.7) If the patient can sit at all, and if so for how long?

(4.8) If the patient cannot stand and/or sit upright for six to eight hours, what is the reason?

(4.9) Does the disability or impairment require the patient to lie down during the day?　Yes　No

(4.10) If the answer is yes then please explain why?

(4.11) How far can the patient walk non stop?

(4.12) How much weight can the patient lift and carry during an
eight hour period?

Less than 5 lb.   5- 10 lb.   11-20 lb.

21-50 lb.   Over 50lb.

Please check the frequency with which the patient can perform
the following activities:

Percentage of Time	Rarely 0-29%	Frequently 30-70%	Consistently 71-100%
Reach Up Above Shoulders			
Reach Down to Waist Level			
Reach Down Towards Floor			
Carefully Handle Objects			
Able to Squat			
Able to Kneel			

(4.13) When do you think the patient will be able to resume any type of work?

Approximate Date: Month _____ Day _____ 20 _____

☐ Indefinitely   ☐ Never

(5) Does the patient have any complaints of pain?   ☐ Yes   ☐ No

(5.1) If the patient has pain, what is the nature of the pain?

(5.2) How frequent is the pain?

☐ Continuous   ☐ Hourly   ☐ Daily   ☐ Weekly

(5.3) How would you describe the level of pain?

☐ Mild   ☐ Moderate   ☐ Severe

(6) Is the patient a suitable candidate for a rehabilitation program?

☐ Yes   ☐ No

(7) Mental Condition:

(8) Is the patient competent to endorse checks and direct the use of the proceeds thereof?   Yes   No

(9) Remarks:

_____

Date: _____ _____ _____
              Month   Day   Year

Name of Physician (Please Print) _____

Signature _____ Degree _____

Street Address _____

_____
        City   State   Zip Code

Physician's Stamp

If you apply for disability in person, remember you have requested disability benefits because you are too sick or injured to work. You need to be completely honest about your condition.

I have read heart breaking stories where judges have denied disability claims for various subjective reasons. One woman claimed she was denied disability benefits because she had her nails polished. She claimed the judge surmised that since she was able to paint her nails than she should be able to work. Whereas, I was told by another individual that the judge ruled against her because she had a Facebook account. Remember, if it is difficult for some of your friends and family to understand the scope of your illness then the same may hold true with our court system.

I have learned from others that it is best not to alter your everyday appearance when you attend your disability benefit court date. If you are a woman who usually feels too sick to wear cosmetics, blow dry your hair or press your clothes then your appearance in court should not be any different. Unfortunately, your physical appearance may extremely deceive others about your internal day to day health struggles. Bottom line, I feel it is best to show up to court and display your everyday appearance.

To qualify for disability benefits under Social Security you must be totally disabled. Benefits are not given for a short-term disability or partial disability.

The following is a list of adult impairments that are applicable to apply for Social Security Disability Benefits. Under each impairment there are numerous impairment subcategories:

Musculoskeletal System	Special Senses and Speech
Digestive System	Genitourinary Impairments
Cardiovascular System	Skin Disorders
Congenital Disorders	Neurological
Endocrine Disorders	Respiratory System
Hematological Disorders	Malignant Neoplastic Diseases
Mental Disorders	Immune System Disorders[1]

Every person that files a Social Security Disability Application is responsible to show medical evidence that validates the severity of the impairment. A Social Security Disability Insurance application check list is provided on the next page. This check list will help you confirm you have collected your medical information. You should have all of your medical information available before you apply for Social Security Disability Insurance . An approximate 70% of all SSDI applications are denied the first time. [2] You will mostly likely become part of the 70% statistic if your SSDI application is not completed correct.

The Statement of Attending Physician form and the Statement From Friends and Family form provided on the previous pages may help you expedite your Social Security

Disability Application. You are far more likely to have your SSDI application approved the first time if you have a completed and detailed application. Please remember, your financial well being may rely on this one application.

✔	CHECK LIST FOR YOUR SSDI APPLICATION
	Information about your impairment from a licensed physician
	Your medical report
	Your medical history
	Your clinical records (This would include results of your mental status and physical examination)
	All your lab reports (Lab Reports would include CT Scans, Blood Pressure, MRI)
	Your licensed physician's diagnosis of your disease or injury
	A treatment plan (The treatment plan should include a prognosis)
	A statement from your physician of what type of work you can do despite your impairment
	You may also include other statements about your medical condition from your physician assistant, chiropractor, educational personnel, public and private social welfare agencies, friends, family, caregivers, neighbors, clergy and spouses.

CHAPTER FOUR

Questions and Answers on Disability Benefits

HypoGal ®

You are most likely reading this book because you or someone you know has experienced a disability. You realize how overwhelming it can be to navigate government disability benefits.

My wife receives numerous questions about disability benefits through her HypoGal website and her HypoGal blog. I have decided it would help others if I replied to many of the frequently asked questions.

QUESTION: How do you apply for Government Disability Benefits?

ANSWER: To apply for Government Disability Benefits you need to complete Disability Form 3368. You can find this form on the Social Security Administrations website, www.SSA.Gov.

Once you are on the Social Security Administration web site you will need to click on several links before you can reach the SSDI application. The first link you need to click on is the Benefits. The Benefits tab can be found in the third column at the top of the page.

After you click on, "Benefits" a drop down window will appear. The third column in the benefit drop box is labeled," Apply". Underneath the Apply header you can click on, Apply Online for Disability.

The Apply Online for Disability link will take you to the Benefit Application page. Once you are on the Benefit Application web page you can view a one minute video that gives you an overview on how to complete your application.

After you watch the video you can continue online to complete your Disability Benefit application. The web page states it should take you ten to thirty minutes to complete the SSDI application. However, I have found that it may take you hours to complete the online application.

You are not required to complete your online application in one session. You may save your application and complete the application when it is best for you. Once you have completed the application you are able to submit your application online directly to Social Security.

If you are unable to complete an online application you can schedule a phone appointment. During the phone appointment a Social Security representative will assist you with your Social Security Disability Insurance application.[1]

QUESTION: What are the statistics of being approved for Social Security Disability Benefits the first time I apply?

ANSWER: 70% of Social Security Disability Benefits applicants are denied the first time. Many of these applications are denied because the application was not complete. If you want your SSDI application to be approved the first time it is extremely important that you provide concise and detailed information of your disability.[2]

QUESTION: How much money will I receive monthly from Social Security Disability Benefits?

ANSWER: The average Social Security Disability Insurance monthly payment in 2013 is $1,132. The maximum monthly amount of SSDI in 2013 is $2,533.[3]

QUESTION: Are my Social Security Disability benefits taxed?

ANSWER: Your Social Security Disability Income (SSDI) is not taxable if half of your SSDI and all your other income is less than:

$25,000 if you filed as single, head of household, or married filing separately, and you and your spouse have not lived together during the year.

$32,000 if you are married and filing jointly.

Up to 85% of your SSDI is taxable if half of your SSDI and all your other income is more than:

$34,000 if you filed as single, head of household, or married filing separately, and you and your spouse have not lived together during the year.

$44,000 if you are married and filing jointly.[4]

QUESTION: Will my Private Disability Benefits be taxed?

ANSWER: How you pay your private disability policy will effect whether your benefits are taxed. If your disability payment is paid through your company payroll then your benefits are taxable. However, if your disability benefits were paid from personal after tax dollars then your disability benefits are tax free.[4]

QUESTION: Is a person able to receive funds from private disability insurance and government disability benefits at the same time?

ANSWER: Yes, a person may receive both private disability insurance and Social Security Disability Benefits.[5]

QUESTION: If I do not work can I obtain private disability insurance?

ANSWER: Private disability insurance is structured for individuals with a job. Whereas, critical illness insurance is best suited for spouses of high wage earners.

If you are the spouse of a high wage earner your spouse most likely cannot afford to spend time away from work to care for you. The critical illness insurance enables you to receive a lump sum payment. The lump sum payment can help you pay for in-home care, child care and medical bills.

Unfortunately, many spouses have been touched by an illness. The recovery from a heart attack, cancer or stroke may take months. The protection of a critical illness insurance policy would allow your family not to be financial stressed by the burden of additional medical bills.[6]

QUESTION: What should I look for in a private disability policy?

ANSWER:
- First decide if you need your policy to begin 90 days or 180 days after you become disabled. A longer wait period will lower your premium.

- Make sure the policy you purchase is, "own occupation". Own occupation means if you cannot do your current job the policy will pay you. If the policy states,"any occupation" it means you can perform any job.

- You should decide how much money you will need each month. The amount of your monthly payout will affect the cost of your premium.

- Make sure your policy provides coverage until the age of 65. At the age of 65 your government benefits will begin. You should also check to make sure that your policy guarantees an annual renewal.

- You need to make sure that your are assigned the correct risk assessment. Your job risk assessment is one of the factors that determines your premium.,7

QUESTION: How do I obtain private disability insurance?

ANSWER: You need to find a disability insurance broker that is well versed in different disability policies. It is best to use an insurance broker because you are able to compare different disability policy options.

When you are looking for an insurance disability broker ask friends and family for their input. You should also use an insurance broker that specializes in disability insurance.

You should let your insurance broker know that you are only interested in purchasing disability insurance from an insurance company with a AAA rating from Standard & Poor's.

If you would like to be directed to a reputable disability insurance broker then you can send a request to David@HypoGal.com or you can fill out the request form on the following page.

Please complete the form and then fold the form on dotted lines. After I receive your request I will refer you to a reputable and experienced licensed broker that can address your disability insurance needs.

Please fold on the dotted lines and then mail to:
Real Deal Exchange Corp.
23052-H Alicia Parkway, PMB #336
Mission Viejo, CA. 92692

You can read about HypoGal at www.HypoGal.com. You can also read about HypoGal's life with a chronic illness at blog.HypoGal.com

Fold Here

I am interested in learning more about disability insurance. Please provide my information to an experienced disability insurance agent.

Name _____ Age _____

Address _____

Phone Number _____ Best Time To Reach Me _____

EMail Address _____

Fold Here

HypoGal

Thank you for purchasing the HypoGal book.
A portion of all book profits will be used to establish a fund for the chronically ill.

NOTES

HypoGal ®

CHAPTER ONE

1. Paul Hsieh, Contributor, Is Concierge Medicine The Correct Choice For You? Forbes 3/27/2013 @ 8:00AM, http://www.forbes.com/sites/paulhsieh/2013/03/27/is-concierge-medicine-the-correct-choice-for-you/

2. John Waggoner, Is a high-deductible health plan right for you? USA TODAY 2:06 a.m. EDT, September 24, 2013, http://www.usatoday.com/story/money/personalfinance/2013/09/24/high-deductible-health-care-plans/2848181/

3. Sarah Cliff, Washington Post, An average ER visit costs more than an average month's rent Published: March 2 at 9:43 am, http://www.washingtonpost.com/blogs/wonkblog/wp/2013/03/02/an-average-er-visit-costs-more-than-an-average-months-rent/

4. United States Department of Labor, Secretary of Labor Thomas E. Perez, Health Plans and Benefits, http://www.dol.gov/dol/topic/health-plans/cobra.htm

CHAPTER TWO

1. Social Security Disability Benefits, SSA Publication No. 05-10029, ICN 456000, June 2012, http://www.ssa.gov/pubs/ EN-05-10029.pdf page 4

2. Council For Disability Awareness, The 2013 Council for Disability Awareness Long Term Disability Claims Review http://www.disabilitycanhappen.org/research/CDA_LTD_ Claims_Survey_2013.asp

3. Social Security Administration, Receiving Medicare and disability benefits Updated 01/02/2013 10:26 AM, http:// ssa-custhelp.ssa.gov/app/answers/detail/a_id/155/kw/ statistics%20on%20becoming%20disabled%20from%20 illness

4. Social Security Administration SSA Publication No. 05-10024, ICN 454930 February 2013 http://www.ssa.gov/ pubs/EN-05-10024.pdf pages 11-12

5. Social Security Administration, SSA Publication No. 05-10024, ICN 454930 February 2013 http://www.ssa.gov/ pubs/EN-05-10024.pdf pages 5-6

6. Social Security Administration, Benefit amount based on changes to disability, Updated 03/27/2013 10:00 AM | ID# 384,http://ssa-custhelp.ssa.gov/app/answers/detail/a_id/ 384/kw/The%20monthly%20amount%20of%20SSDI%20 I%20received%20would%20not%20be%20based%20on%20 the%20severity%20of%20the%20disability.%20Also%2

C%20if%20my%20disability%20progressed%20my%20
monthly%20Social%20Security%20Disability%20
Insurance%20would%20remain%20the%20same

7. Social Security Administration, Computing workers' compensation offset before paying retroactive benefits, Updated 04/11/2013 10:21 AM | ID# 595 http://ssa-custhelp. ssa.gov/app/answers/detail/a_id/595/kw/The%20 monthly%20amount%20of%20SSDI%20I%20received%20 would%20not%20be%20based%20on%20the%20severity %20of%20the%20disability.%20Also%2C%20if%20 my%20disability%20progressed%20my%20monthly%20 Social%20Security%20Disability%20Insurance%20would %20remain%20the%20same

8. Social Security Administration, You May Be Able To Get Supplemental Security Income (SSI), SSA Publication No. 05-11069, 2013 http://www.socialsecurity.gov/pubs/EN-05-11069.pdf page 2

9. Social Security Administration, Supplemental Security Income amount, Updated 07/16/2013 03:47 PM | ID# 85 http://ssa-custhelp.ssa.gov/app/answers/detail/a_id/85/~/ supplemental-security-income-amount

10. Social Security Administration, Effects of private disability on Social Security benefits Updated 05/31/2013, 03:51 AM | ID# 154 http://ssa-custhelp.ssa.gov/app/answers/detail/a_ id/154/~/effects-of-private-disability-on-social-security-benefits

11. Social Security Administration, Disability Benefits, SSA Publication No. 05-10029 ICN 456000, June 2012 ,http://www.ssa.gov/pubs/EN-05-10029.pdf page 4

12. Social Security Administration, Disability Benefits, SSA Publication No. 05-10029 ICN 456000, June 2012 ,http://www.ssa.gov/pubs/EN-05-10029.pdf pages 9-10

13. Social Security Administration, Disability Benefits, SSA Publication No. 05-10029 ICN 456000, June 2012 ,http://www.ssa.gov/pubs/EN-05-10029.pdf page 4

14. The Motley Fool, Insurance Center, What factors should I consider before buying private disability insurance? http://www.fool.com/insurancecenter/disability/disability05.htm

15. Social Security Administration, Disability Benefits, SSA Publication No. 05-10029 ICN 456000, June 2012 ,http://www.ssa.gov/pubs/EN-05-10029.pdf pages 9-10

16. AARP, What IS the Doughnut Hole? http://doughnuthole.aarp.org

17. Social Security Administration, Model Fee Agreement Language http://www.ssa.gov/representation/model_fee_agreement_language.htm

18. Social Security Administration, Disability Benefits, SSA Publication NO. 05-10029, ICN 45600, June 2012, http://www.ssa.gov/pubs/EN-05-10029.pdf page 12

19. Social Security Administration, When Social Security disability benefits end, Updated 09/03/2013 04:54 PM |

ID# 458 http://ssa-custhelp.ssa.gov/app/answers/detail/a_id/458/kw/statistics%20on%20becoming%20disabled%20from%20illness

20. Dan Mangan | Health Care Reporter Medical Bills Are the Biggest Cause of US Bankruptcies: Study, CNBC, Published: Tuesday, 25 Jun 2013 | 2:29 PM ET http://www.cnbc.com/id/100840148

CHAPTER 3

1. Social Security Administration, Medical / Professional Relationships, Disability Evaluation Under Social Security: http://www.ssa.gov/disability/professionals/bluebook/AdultListings.htm

2. Social Security Administration, Disability Benefits, SSA Publication NO. 05-10029, ICN 45600, June 2012, http://www.ssa.gov/pubs/EN-05-10029.pdf page 12

CHAPTER 4

1. Social Security Administration , Apply for Social Security disability benefits, Updated 10/09/2013, 10:56 AM | ID# 326, http://ssa-custhelp.ssa.gov/app/answers/detail/a_id/326/kw/statistics%20on%20becoming%20disabled%20from%20illness

2. Social Security Administration, 2013 Selected Data From Social Security's Disability Program http://www.ssa.gov/oact/STATS/dibStat.html

3. Social Security Administration, 2013 Social Security Changes, Fact Sheet http://www.socialsecurity.gov/pressoffice/factsheets/colafacts2013.htm

4. Internal Revenue Service, Regular & Disability Benefits, Page Last Reviewed or Updated: 19-Dec-2012 http://www.irs.gov/Help-&-Resources/Tools-&-FAQs/FAQs-for-Individuals/Frequently-Asked-Tax-Questions-&-Answers/Social-Security-Income/Regular-&-Disability-Benefits/Regular-&-Disability-Benefits

5. Social Security Administration, Effects of private disability on Social Security benefits, Updated 05/31/2013 03:51 AM | ID# 154, http://ssa-custhelp.ssa.gov/app/answers/detail/a_id/154/kw/statistics%20on%20becoming%20disabled%20from%20illness

6. Elizabeth O'Brien, The Wall Street Journal, Market Watch, August 8, 2013, 6:31 a.m. EDTIs critical-illness insurance worth the money? http://www.marketwatch.com/story/is-critical-illness-insurance-worth-the-money-2013-08-08

7. Paul Sullivan, Weighing the Odds of Disability, for Insurance Purposes, The New York Times, October 19, 2012 http://www.nytimes.com/2012/10/20/your-money/life-and-disability-insurance/determining-if-disability-insurance-is-necessary.html

GLOSSARY

HypoGal ®

Co-pay: In the United States, copayment or copay is a payment defined in the insurance policy and paid by the insured person each time a medical service is accessed. It is technically a form of coinsurance, but is defined differently in health insurance where a coinsurance is a percentage payment after the deductible up to a certain limit. It must be paid before any policy benefit is payable by an insurance company. Co-payments do not usually contribute towards any policy out-of-pocket maxima whereas coinsurance payments do.

COBRA: The Consolidated Omnibus Budget Reconciliation Act (COBRA) gives workers and their families who lose their health benefits the right to choose to continue group health benefits provided by their group health plan for limited periods of time under certain circumstances such as voluntary or involuntary job loss, reduction in the hours worked, transition between jobs, death, divorce, and other life events. Qualified individuals may be required to pay the entire premium for coverage up to 102 percent of the cost to the plan. COBRA generally requires that group health plans sponsored by employers with 20 or more employees in the prior year offer employees and their families the opportunity for a temporary extension of health coverage (called continuation coverage) in certain instances where coverage under the plan would otherwise end.

Health Maintenance Organization (HMO): is a type of health insurance that has a list of providers, such as doctors, medical groups, hospitals, and labs.

You must receive all of your health care from the providers on this list. This list is called a network. Usually you have a primary doctor, who is part of a medical group that has a contract with the HMO. Your primary doctor is the doctor who will manage your care. If you need to see specialists, medical tests, or be in the hospital, your doctor and the medical group must approve the service.

Usually you pay a fee, called a co-pay, for each service. You may also have a yearly deductible. This is the amount you must pay each year before your HMO pays for any services. An HMO has a service area. You must live or work in one of the zip codes in the service area to join the HMO.

HypoGal: Lisa G. created HypoGal to bring attention to Sheehan's Syndrome. Sheehan's Syndrome is a rare disease of the pituitary gland that is frequently misdiagnosed. The pituitary gland is a burnt red, soft, oval pea sized gland that is located at the base of our brain. The pituitary gland is often referred to as the master gland. It is referred to as the master gland because the pituitary releases hormones that control almost all of our endocrine system. The master gland (pituitary gland) sends signals to our other glands to produce hormones that regulate growth in childhood, control our metabolism, libido, fertility, emotions, sexual maturity and muscle tone.

Internal Revenue Service (IRS): is the revenue service of the United States federal government. The agency is a bureau of the Department of the Treasury, and is under the immediate direction of the Commissioner of Internal Revenue. The IRS is responsible for collecting taxes and the interpretation and enforcement of the Internal Revenue Code.

Medicare: is the federal health insurance program for people who are 65 or older, certain younger people with disabilities, and people with End-Stage Renal Disease (permanent kidney failure requiring dialysis or a transplant, sometimes called ESRD).

Preferred Provider Organization (PPO): is good plan for people who want to see medical providers without a prior approval from their health plan or medical group and may not want to choose a primary care doctor.

You receive most of your health care from a network of doctors and other providers. You are allowed to go outside of the network for some care and pay a higher cost. You usually pay a yearly deductible and a percentage of the bill.

Private Disability Insurance (PDI): Insurance plan that can be purchased to provide benefits when illness or injury prevents employment.

Sheehan's Syndrome: is caused by severe blood loss during or after childbirth. The blood loss during and post childbirth can be particularly damaging to the pituitary gland. The loss of blood to the pituitary gland may destroy hormone-producing tissue. When necrosis of the pituitary gland occurs the pituitary may lose some or all of its function.

The disease, Sheehan's Syndrome is named after Dr. Harold Leeming Sheehan. It was in 1937 that Dr. Sheehan's complete concept of the syndrome was reviewed. He emphasized that during pregnancy the pituitary becomes enlarged, but its blood supply becomes diminished. If a woman hemorrhages during childbirth it causes a severe drop in blood pressure (hypotension) and may damage the pituitary. A simple way to understand this concept is the loss of blood (hemorrhaging) to the pituitary creates an infarct, (stroke) in the pituitary. The infarct causes part or all of the pituitary to stop functioning. This damage to the pituitary gland can happen immediately after childbirth or the pituitary gland can gradually decline in function.

Supplemental Nutrition Assistance Program (SNAP): offers nutrition assistance to millions of eligible, low-income individuals and families and provides economic benefits to communities. SNAP is the largest program in the domestic hunger safety net. The Food and Nutrition Service works with State agencies, nutrition educators, and neighborhood and faith-based organizations to ensure that those eligible for nutrition assistance can make informed decisions about applying for the program and can access benefits. FNS also works with State partners and the retail community to improve program administration and ensure program integrity.

Social Security: In the United States, Social Security is the Old-Age, Survivors, and Disability Insurance (OASDI) federal program. The original Social Security Act (1935) and the current version of the Act, as amended, encompass several social welfare and social insurance programs. Social Security is funded through payroll taxes called Federal Insurance Contributions Act tax (FICA) and/or Self Employed Contributions Act Tax, (SECA). Tax deposits are collected by the Internal Revenue Service, IRS and are formally entrusted to the Federal Old-Age and Survivors Insurance Trust Fund, the Federal Disability Insurance Trust Fund, the Federal Hospital Insurance Trust Fund, or the Federal Supplementary Medical Insurance Trust Fund which comprise the Social Security Trust Fund.

Social Security Disability Insurance (SSDI): A benefit paid to you and certain members of your family if you are "insured," meaning that you worked long enough and paid Social Security taxes.

Supplemental Security Income (SSI): is a Federal income supplement program funded by general tax revenues (not Social Security taxes). The program is designed to help aged, blind, and disabled people, who have little or no income. The program provides funds to meet basic needs for food, clothing, and shelter.

ABOUT THE AUTHOR

David Gorlick and his wife Lisa (a.k.a.) HypoGal have been married since 1996. David is from the Worcester, MA and currently resides in Southern CA. David and Lisa enjoy raising their wonderful daughters.

The author David Gorlick is not a medical expert nor a legal expert in the field of Social Security, however he wanted to compile this financially imperative information to help guide others to the financial resources available to those with living with disabilities.

After spending more than a decade researching Social Security benefits, navigating financial hurdles, confirming insurance claims and living with a wife who has a long term chronic illness, he felt the need to create a form of public awareness for those who live with a long term disability. This led him to write HypoGal and Disability Benefits which was derived from his own personal experiences and may not be applicable to your diagnosed situation.

This book was written with the intent to help you explore your medical disability insurance needs. For more information visit; www.hypogal.com

A CALL TO ACTION

HypoGal ®

Please help spread the word about HypoGal's efforts to help navigate life with a chronic illness.

If you belong to Facebook please, "Like" HypoGal's Facebook Page

I invite you to follow, HypoGal on Twitter

You can also subscribe to the YouTube HypoGal Network Channel

Your input provides valuable guidance so please review this book.

www.ingramcontent.com/pod-product-compliance
Lightning Source LLC
Chambersburg PA
CBHW060511280326
41933CB00014B/2927